The Common Cents of Continuous Improvement Systems

By Larry Ibbetson of Ibbetson
Performance Consulting LLC

DEDICATION

To my wife, Mary Lee, and children Larry, Korryn, Andrea and Ron, son-in-law Todd, daughter-in-law Kelly, grandchildren RJ, Kayla (Blu) and Ella for their patience with me in working on this effort.

Table of Contents:

INTRODUCTION

A Continuous Improvement System (CIS), also known as Continuous Process Improvement (CPI), is an ongoing effort to improve processes, products, or services through incremental changes. It is a systematic and structured approach that involves identifying areas for improvement, developing strategies to address them, implementing those strategies, and measuring the results. Continuous Improvement is a key component of many quality management systems, including Total Quality Management (TQM), Lean Manufacturing, and Six Sigma.

According to the Institute for Healthcare Improvement (IHI), Continuous Improvement is defined as "a systematic approach to improving health care processes and outcomes that involves ongoing efforts to achieve incremental improvements over time" (IHI, 2021).

The International Organization for Standardization (ISO) also defines Continuous Improvement as "recurring activity to increase the ability to fulfill requirements" (ISO, 2015).[i]

Continuous Improvement is widely used across different industries, including manufacturing, healthcare, and service industries, to increase efficiency, reduce waste, and improve customer satisfaction.

If you feel frustrated with repetitive issues in your business that consume your time, energy, and money then this book is for you. Sometimes you may feel you are on a treadmill of never-ending repetitive business process issues. There is a commonsense approach to getting on top of these issues. There is a simple and easy system you can employ today, without investing a lot of money, that will create a huge change in how you perform the business processes that have been causing you headaches. This book is for Business Owners, Managers, CFOs, and anyone in an organization that wants to put their company on a path to achieve their objectives. This book will show you how to start your Continuous Improvement System.

I did not misspell "Cents" in my title. The "Cents" is a reference to what you invested in purchasing this book. A "Return on Investment", in terms of Performance Improvement after implementing the ideas in this book, is what I would expect from any reader that understands these benefits. Of course, only a successful implementation of a Continuous Improvement System will ultimately determine whether any company will achieve that ROI. It is my hope that the reader will benefit from the insights contained in the following pages and launch a Continuous Improvement System that delivers on the promise presented by such a System.

Scholars have researched many of the most successful companies in a variety of fields and have found a common theme. They had a defining moment. That moment occurred when they faced situations that threatened their very existence. They were forced to change or die. They were forced to make a choice as to how to survive. Making that choice is viewed by many as "Strategy". Every Strategy involves making decisions, choices about how to proceed. In this book I am asking you to make a choice.

This book is intended for the businesses that have not started a real Continuous Improvement System. Did you know there are roughly 320 million small businesses in the global economy today? A very large percentage of these companies have not yet begun their journey using a Continuous Improvement System. Most of the 60,000

Multinational Companies in the global economy have mature Continuous Improvement Systems. They use advanced techniques like Lean Six/DMAIC Principles, Agile/Scrum, 5 Whys Root Cause Analysis, Design of Experiment/Taguchi Methods, and Ishigawa Diagrams to enhance their processes in their Continuous Improvement Systems.

The initiation of a Continuous Improvement System is the start of a never-ending journey. You must develop the mindset and company culture to support the growth of this System within your business. The core ideas are to determine your Key Performance Indicators (KPIs), measure these KPIs, analyze the results, and make small incremental changes that will make a huge improvement over time. Before such an effort can be undertaken some capabilities and infrastructure must be in place. This includes your "processes" being documented. You must have a baseline written and documented process to begin a Continuous Improvement System. A process is any series of steps designed to output a result that is key to delivering value to your customer. Training to ensure that process is followed by everyone involved in that process is a key perquisite before starting the system. You will also need the ability to collect actionable information about that process. The ability to clearly define any problems found and to make small but meaningful changes are a critical element of this system.

Not every change will result in improvement. However, every change will yield additional information. Remember Thomas Edison, the inventor and founder of General Electric, who replied when asked why he had failed 10,000 times trying to create the lightbulb. He said, "I have not failed 10,000 times -I've successfully found 10,000 ways that will not work."

My name is Larry Ibbetson. I started in Manufacturing Operations when I was a teenager working for our family-owned Electronics Contract Manufacturing Company before the concept of Contract Manufacturing was created. This was back in the late 1960s before going to college in 1973. I have a wealth of experience and knowledge that I want to share with you.

Starting at that early age in business provided me with a perspective that has proven to be very valuable in my career. I received an education in how to perform processes that were critical to a product. We strove to attain consistent and improving process results while minimizing or eliminating process variation. I learned the value of efficient output, the critical nature of product quality, and the high expectations of customers.

I have founded two businesses, worked in Aerospace, Medical Devices, Automotive, Real Estate Sales and Marketing, Industrial, Consulting, and Sales/Distribution businesses. I have consulted in a variety of business marketplaces both in the US and Internationally in Europe and Asia. I have seen how to do things both correctly and incorrectly. I have learned that making mistakes is the hallmark of learning. However, you must learn from mistakes. I have been enlightened to the fact that there are really no failures. You either succeed or you learn.

If you haven't started your Continuous Improvement journey yet it is my hope that in reading this book, I will have aroused your curiosity and provoked you towards action. Continuous Improvement can be made into a common sense and simple approach to get started. It is an approach, a mindset, a scientific system, a methodology for getting improvement into any process. We all deal with processes every day. Doesn't it make sense to create a path for being better at what you do every day?

By implementing these ideas, you should increase your profits, improve your customer satisfaction with your services or products, and build a positive, ever improving company culture that attracts customers and employees.

CHAPTER 1:

THE DAILY STRUGGLE

A lot of Business Owners and Managers, that are responsible for the outcomes of their enterprises, are in a daily struggle to resolve problems after they happen. This is the never-ending cycle of firefighting. Doesn't it make sense to develop a plan that prevents these problems from happening in the first place? A Continuous Improvement System is a simple, scientific method-based process, that will allow you to systematically address problems and improve daily.

Continuous Improvement is based on the concept that if you make small changes, on a consistent basis, you will improve long term performance. A Continuous Improvement System will create momentum for your business to deliver increased value to your customers, higher margins for your business, and create an internal culture where your employees feel they are part of an ever-improving organization. A Continuous Improvement System can be the fabric of your Company's Culture, intertwined in how every process is controlled, measured, and improved on a repetitive basis.

Did you know that if you improved 1% every day this would add up to a 37 times improvement over the course of 1 year? An astounding 75% of Change Initiatives fail either outright or that they fail to achieve their desired outcomes. Large changes have a higher probability of failure. The risk mitigation of setting up a system that results in small, incremental changes, driving momentum towards key business objectives should be obvious to all.

What is a Continuous Improvement System in Business Operations? In the simplest form it is an intentional system that collects performance data, analyzes the results, allows for design changes to processes and performs the cycle again and again. It is a mindset that everyone in the business should adopt.

Continuous Improvement is the mechanism that allows businesses to make positive changes to how things are done in a process. These changes are based on feedback using the data generated by business or manufacturing processes. A process is any predetermined set of steps to achieve a desired outcome. Everything we do in business should be considered a process if done in a repetitive manner.

In a business environment, every repetitive action can be considered a process. A process is a series of steps or activities that are performed in a specific order to achieve a particular goal or outcome. Processes can be found in every aspect of a business, from manufacturing and production to customer service and sales. Documenting these processes is essential to ensure consistency, efficiency, and quality in the delivery of products or services.

To document a process, it is important to identify the steps involved, the resources required, the roles and responsibilities of those involved, and any potential risks or issues that may arise. This information can be captured in a process map or flowchart, which provides a visual representation of the steps involved in the process.

A process map or flowchart should include the following elements:

1. Start and end points: Identify the starting point and endpoint of the process.

2. Process steps: Document each step involved in the process, using clear and concise language.

3. Decision points: Identify any decision points or branching paths in the process, where different actions may be taken depending on the circumstances.

4. Roles and responsibilities: Clearly define the roles and responsibilities of those involved in the process, including any decision-makers or approvers.

5. Resources: Identify any resources required to complete the process, such as equipment, materials, or software.

6. Risks and issues: Identify any potential risks or issues that may arise during the process and outline the steps to mitigate or address these risks.

By documenting processes in this way, businesses can ensure that all employees are following the same procedures, resulting in consistent and high-quality outcomes. It also allows for continuous improvement, as businesses can identify areas where processes can be streamlined or optimized to increase efficiency and reduce costs.

Documenting processes is also essential for compliance and regulatory purposes. Many industries have strict regulations and guidelines that businesses must follow to ensure the safety and well-being of their customers and employees. By documenting processes, businesses can demonstrate that they are following these regulations and guidelines, reducing the risk of legal or financial penalties.

Every repetitive action in a business environment can be considered a process. Documenting these processes is essential to ensure consistency, efficiency, and quality in the delivery of products or services. By identifying the steps involved, the resources required, and any potential risks or issues, businesses can ensure that all employees are following the same procedures, resulting in consistent and high-quality outcomes. It also allows for continuous improvement and ensures compliance with regulatory requirements. Some companies may employ "self-audit" programs that periodically verify that the processes are accurate and are being followed by the employees executing these functions. Drift from the baseline process is an inherent characteristic of process life cycle. It happens when sometimes subtle changes are adopted by the employees and over time these become an undocumented part of workflow. Some call this growing undocumented drift the "hidden factory". Minimizing the effects of the hidden factory is a key objective of any Continuous Improvement System.

The term "hidden factory" refers to the inefficiencies and waste that exist within a manufacturing process that are not immediately visible or apparent. These inefficiencies can include defects, scrap, rework, and other non-value-added activities that can negatively impact productivity and profitability. The term was first coined by Armand V. Feigenbaum, a quality control expert, in his book "Total Quality Control" in 1951.[ii]

CHAPTER 2:

HISTORY OF CONTINUOUS IMPROVEMENT

If you ask most people about Continuous Improvement, you will most likely get a reference to Kaizen, a Japanese concept. Kaizen comes from two Japanese words Kai and Zen. Kai is the Japanese word for change. Zen is the Japanese word for good. Kaizen is often referred to as the Japanese concept for Continuous Improvement.

It is a myth that Continuous Improvement started as a concept created in Japan. The roots of Continuous Improvement came from a US Department of War initiative in 1940 called Training Within Industry (TWI). It was designed to help less experienced workers help businesses meet the needs of World War II materials production. These workers were replaced after World War II and the benefits and practices of TWI were largely forgotten in the US.

It was introduced into Japan and Europe after World War II to help rebuild the devasted economies post war. In Japan it was embraced by several companies including Toyota. Toyota developed it's TPS system based on the elimination of waste in any process or system. W. Edwards Deming and General MacArthur both played keys roles in rebuilding Japan's industrial base after World War II. Deming's use of PDCA cycle is a driving practice of Continuous Improvement. PDCA is the acronym for Plan, Do, Check, and Act. When combined with accurate process data this becomes the tools that enables a Continuous Improvement System.

W. Edwards Deming was a renowned statistician and quality control expert. He was a strong advocate of the PDCA cycle and was instrumental in popularizing its use in quality management. Deming began using the PDCA cycle in the 1950s as part of his work in Japan to help rebuild their manufacturing industry after World War II. He emphasized the importance of the PDCA cycle as a framework for continuous improvement and quality management, and his teachings had a profound impact on Japanese industry and later with American industry as well.

Deming's work in Japan and his emphasis on the PDCA cycle helped to establish the foundation for what would later become known as Total Quality Management (TQM) and Lean Manufacturing. His teachings and principles continue to be influential in the field of quality management. They have had a profound impact on the development of modern quality management practices. Deming began using the PDCA cycle in the 1950s as part of his work in Japan to help rebuild their manufacturing industry. He emphasized the importance of the PDCA cycle as a framework for continuous improvement and quality management, and his teachings had a profound impact on the development of modern quality management practices. While Deming did not invent the PDCA cycle, he was instrumental in popularizing its use and demonstrating its effectiveness in improving quality and productivity in manufacturing processes.

Today there are many "tools" in the proverbial toolbox that can be enlisted to help drive Continuous Improvement Systems. They include Lean, Agile, Six Sigma, TQM, Kanban, Kaizen Events, 5S, and many others. These tools are geared for measuring defects, driving changes, eliminating waste, creating clean and orderly work areas, solving problems, reducing inventory, reducing wait times, and optimization of cycle times.

These tools and the Continuous Improvement System are viewed as critical infrastructure for sustainable growing companies. There is a cultural aspect to Continuous Improvement. To make this system effective it must become a mindset for the people living and using it.

Continuous Improvement can be applied to any process, any business, any location, and any culture. It is highly versatile and adaptable. In today's environment if you are not utilizing a Continuous Improvement System you are at a huge disadvantage to your competition that does use it. It is a system that can be instituted in the smallest of operations to the largest.

Prerequisites to institute a Continuous Improvement System are a Strategic Plan and a set of Key Performance Indicators. You will need a way of collecting and measuring process results, a realistic target and timetable for changes, a written baseline process, a company policy and culture to follow the processes, and a management commitment for time, resources, and the empowerment for the teams to make changes based on the data.

I have included this Chapter on the History of Continuous Improvement not to impress you, the reader, that I have researched the origins of this concept but to show how critical this approach is. The Department of War, at the early stages of World War II, understood the need to put a program together that would take untrained, replacement workers and prepare them to take on the critical tasks necessary to ramp up wartime production. In essence, the life of the USA was at stake. Failure was not an option.

In the postwar rebuilding of the devasted economies of Japan and Europe this program was a critical foundation point. Many companies in Japan adopted these concepts and created a multitude of initiatives that are prevalent in today's business world. Toyota's success was not an accident. It was a commitment to improving their processes and to deliver a higher quality product to their customers. Eliminating waste in any system is basically a commonsense idea. The system of how to do this in an effective manner is the key.

CHAPTER 3:

LET'S START - THE BASICS

How do you start a Continuous Improvement System?

You don't need to be a large corporation with deep financial pockets to fund resources to incorporate a Continuous Improvement System into the company culture. No, a one-person enterprise can start. The critical idea of Continuous Improvement is to start and create a mindset, the way you do things. It doesn't matter where you start, it is the fact that you did start.

It is easy to get overwhelmed by the myriad of programs that have been developed to support and enhance Continuous Improvement, Problem Solving, and New Product Development. There are methodologies like Six Sigma, Agile, Lean, and many others that are employed at many businesses and these are usually introduced when a Company is at a mature stage in their Continuous Improvement journey. As you begin your journey in implementing a Continuous Improvement System you may also employ many of these same programs once you have experience and resources to do so. You can start simply by using commonsense initiatives and begin the process.

Creating, analyzing, and using data is critical to the success of this system. Once you have this data what do you do with it? You review and determine the root causes of failures. You can use Pareto Charts to address the most pressing issues first. A critical point to focus on is do you have the talent in place that can analyze this information and formulate proposed solutions to help resolve the root causes?

You must create an environment where your team is able to try things that may or may not work. This is how improvement is achieved. Not every change will be successful. However, every change will yield more information about the process and that, unto itself, is important.

Another critical point is your attitude about developing a Continuous Improvement System. It is crucial to the success of this effort that you have the proper mindset in setting up this system. If you view finding problems as the keys to improvement you will be starting with the right mindset. Denying or ignoring the issues will lead to failure. The facts are the facts and must be honestly dealt with to solve the root causes.

To create a culture of continuous improvement in a company it involves a commitment to ongoing learning, collaboration, and innovation. Here are some steps that can be taken to create a culture of continuous improvement:

1. Establish a clear vision and mission: The first step in creating a culture of continuous improvement is to establish a clear vision and mission for the company. This includes defining the company's goals, values, and objectives, as well as communicating these to employees.

2. Encourage employee engagement: Encourage employees to participate in continuous improvement initiatives by providing opportunities for feedback, collaboration, and innovation. This can include regular meetings, brainstorming sessions, and training programs.

3. Foster a learning environment: Creating a culture of continuous improvement requires a commitment to ongoing learning and development. Encourage employees to pursue

training and professional development opportunities, provide resources and support to help them do so.

4. Implement a continuous improvement framework: Implement a continuous improvement framework such as PDCA (Plan-Do-Check-Act) or Six Sigma to provide a structured approach to problem-solving and process improvement.

5. Measure progress: Establish key performance indicators (KPIs) to measure progress and track the impact of continuous improvement initiatives. This can include metrics such as customer satisfaction, productivity, and employee engagement.

6. Celebrate successes: Celebrate successes to reinforce the importance of continuous improvement and recognize the efforts of employees. This can include recognition programs, awards, and other incentives.

7. Emphasize leadership commitment: Creating a culture of continuous improvement requires leadership commitment and support. Leaders must be willing to invest time, resources, and energy into continuous improvement initiatives and model the behaviors and values that are essential to a culture of continuous improvement.

Companies can create a culture of continuous improvement that fosters innovation, collaboration, and ongoing learning by following these steps. This can lead to improved productivity, increased customer satisfaction, and a competitive advantage in the marketplace. Creating a culture of continuous improvement is an ongoing process that requires a commitment to ongoing learning, collaboration, and innovation, but the rewards can be significant for both the company and its employees.

CHAPTER 4:

THE RUSSIAN NESTING DOLL VIEW OF PROCESSES

As we have discussed earlier, everything we do on a repetitive basis is a process. A process is a series of steps that produce an outcome. In a Continuous Improvement System your processes must be controlled, measured, analyzed, and improved.

The list of what can be considered a process is virtually unlimited. Examples of Processes:

- Sales
- Marketing
- Revenue by Customer
- Revenue by Product
- Cost by Customer
- Cost by Product
- Advertising
- Finance/Accounting/Reporting
- CAPEX Forecasting
- Budget Management
- Accounts Payable
- Accounts Receivable
- Hiring and Recruiting personnel
- Onboarding
- Training

- Employee Retention
- Procurement of Materials
- Supplier/Vendor Selection and Management
- Receiving Materials
- Inventory Control
- Order Entry
- Order Fulfillment
- Manufacturing Process
- Equipment Utilization
- Equipment Maintenance
- Preventive Maintenance
- Quality Assurance
- Quality Control
- Process Control
- Customer/Patient Complaints
- Customer Returns
- Customer Service
- Field Support
- Program Management
- Customer/Patient Feedback

It is reasonable to say that this list is far from comprehensive. However, it is even more complicated than this! All processes have sub-processes. It can be overwhelming when thinking how far down the rabbit hole you can go with controlling, analyzing, measuring, and improving every facet of the business on a continuing basis. It is as if every process is a Russian Nesting Doll, a series of dolls within dolls.

When drilling down on processes, it is common to find that processes are nested within other processes. This is similar to a Russian nesting doll, where each doll is placed inside another, smaller doll. In the same way, processes can be broken down into smaller and smaller processes that are nested within each other.

For example, a manufacturing process may involve several sub-processes, such as materials handling, assembly, inspection, and packaging. Each of these sub-processes can be broken down further into smaller processes, such as machine setup, quality control, and inventory management. These smaller processes may themselves be broken down into even smaller processes, such as component inspection, machine calibration, and data entry.

The advantage of breaking down processes into smaller processes is that it allows for greater visibility and control over the process. By identifying the individual steps involved in a process and the inputs and outputs of each step, it becomes easier to identify areas where improvements can be made. This can lead to increased efficiency, reduced waste, and improved quality.

However, it is important to remember that the goal of breaking down processes into smaller processes is not to create an overly complex system. Rather, the goal is to create a system that is manageable and effective. It is important to strike a balance between breaking down processes into manageable components and maintaining a holistic view of the process.

By breaking down processes into smaller processes, companies can gain a deeper understanding of their operations and identify areas for improvement. This can lead to increased efficiency, reduced waste, and improved quality. It also allows for greater control and visibility over the process, which can help to ensure that the process is functioning as intended.

The point of this book is to start the Continuous Improvement journey. To start it simply and to start today. How do you know where to start? Go back to your Business Strategy. What are you trying to do as a business? Who are you serving and what is important to them?

KPIs are KEY Performance Indicators for a reason. What determines the priority of which processes are required to be controlled, analyzed, measured, and improved first? It must come from your Business Strategy. What is it that you need to do to be successful? Once you determine the what, you decide the how, develop a plan, and execute that plan. No plan is perfect, you must be ready to adjust the plan based on feedback. That feedback comes from your Continuous Improvement System provided you are measuring the right processes.

Think about Mike Tyson, the former Heavy Weight Boxing Champion's famous quote "Everyone has a plan until they get punched in the mouth." And you will get punched in the mouth by customers, patients, competition, the economy, pandemics, suppliers, your team. You must be flexible and be able to take the punches that will come in business.

A great Business Strategy is clear, achievable, and measurable. You pick the place, time, and how you will execute your strategy. You determine the target customers, you develop the competitive advantages, you determine the marketing and sales approaches, you deliver the product or services, you gauge the customer/patient satisfaction, you course correct to improve your performance. You continually improve your performance by measuring and adjusting the **KEY** Performance Indicators.

CHAPTER 5:

REAL LIFE EXAMPLES

Toyota, as previously discussed, is a great example of a company that achieved higher margins and market share through the implementation of a Continuous Improvement System is Toyota. Toyota is well known for its Toyota Production System (TPS), which is a continuous improvement system that focuses on reducing waste, improving quality, and increasing efficiency.

Toyota's implementation of the TPS has enabled the company to achieve higher margins and market share in the automotive industry. For example, in the 1980s, Toyota's market share in the US was only 8%, compared to 27% for General Motors. However, by the mid-2000s, Toyota's market share had increased to 16%, while General Motors' market share had declined to 25%. During this same period, Toyota's profit margins also increased significantly, from 3% in the early 1990s to over 10% in the mid-2000s (Liker, 2004).

Toyota's success can be attributed to its focus on continuous improvement and its commitment to the TPS. Practices the Toyota TPS utilizes include just-in-time production, kanban systems, and kaizen events, which are designed to eliminate waste, improve quality, and increase efficiency. These practices are supported by a culture of continuous improvement, where all employees are encouraged to identify problems and suggest solutions.

For example, Toyota's just-in-time production system is designed to produce vehicles only when they are needed, reducing inventory and waste. A kanban system helps to manage inventory levels and ensure that materials are available when needed. Kaizen events are used to identify and address problems in the production process, with a focus on continuous improvement.

Through these practices, Toyota has been able to achieve higher margins and market share by reducing costs, improving quality, and increasing efficiency. By focusing on continuous improvement, Toyota has also been able to develop a reputation for producing high-quality, reliable vehicles, which has helped to increase customer loyalty and drive sales.

Toyota's implementation of a Continuous Improvement System, specifically the Toyota Production System, has enabled the company to achieve higher margins and market share in the automotive industry. By focusing on reducing waste, improving quality, and increasing efficiency, Toyota has been able to reduce costs and improve profitability. Additionally, by developing a culture of continuous improvement, Toyota has been able to drive innovation and develop a reputation for producing high-quality, reliable vehicles. [iii]

A good example of a service company that benefited from instituting a Continuous Improvement System is Southwest Airlines. Southwest Airlines is a low-cost airline that operates in the United States. The company has been able to achieve higher margins and market share by focusing on continuous improvement and developing a culture of innovation.

Southwest Airlines' Continuous Improvement System is based on the principles of Lean Manufacturing, which is a methodology that focuses on reducing waste and increasing efficiency. The company has implemented many practices to reduce costs and improve quality.

Southwest Airlines has implemented a just-in-time inventory management system that allows the company to keep inventory levels low and reduce waste. The company also uses standardized work processes to ensure that all employees are following the same procedures, which helps to reduce errors and improve efficiency. Additionally, Southwest Airlines holds continuous improvement events, where employees are encouraged to identify problems and suggest solutions.

In utilizing these practices, Southwest Airlines has been able to achieve higher margins and market share by reducing costs and improving the customer experience. The company has been able to reduce turnaround times for its planes, which has allowed it to operate more flights and increase revenue. Additionally, the company has been able to improve the customer experience by reducing delays and cancellations, which has helped to increase customer loyalty and drive sales.

Southwest Airlines' implementation of a Continuous Improvement System, specifically the principles of Lean Manufacturing, has enabled the company to achieve higher margins and market share in the airline industry. Through the focused efforts on reducing waste, improving efficiency, and developing a culture of innovation, Southwest Airlines has been able to reduce costs and improve the customer experience, which has helped to drive revenue growth and increase market share.[iv]

In Healthcare Virginia Mason Medical Center instituted a Continuous Improvement System resulting in higher margins, happier customers, and increased market share. Virginia Mason Medical Center is a nonprofit regional healthcare system located in Seattle, Washington, USA. The company implemented a Continuous Improvement System based on the principles of Lean Manufacturing, which is a methodology that focuses on reducing waste and increasing efficiency.

Virginia Mason Medical Center's Continuous Improvement System is called the Virginia Mason Production System (VMPS). The VMPS involves practices, including standardized work processes, just-in-time inventory management, and continuous improvement events. The goal of the VMPS is to improve the quality of care, reduce costs, and increase efficiency.

Through the implementation of the VMPS, Virginia Mason Medical Center has been able to achieve higher margins, happier customers, and increased market share. For example, the company has been able to reduce the time it takes to complete medical procedures, which has reduced costs and improved the patient experience. Additionally, the company has been able to reduce the number of errors and complications, which has improved patient safety and reduced costs.

The VMPS has also helped Virginia Mason Medical Center to increase market share by developing a reputation for high-quality care. The company has been recognized for its commitment to quality, innovation, and has received numerous awards and accolades for its efforts.

Virginia Mason Medical Center's implementation of a Continuous Improvement System, specifically the Virginia

Mason Production System, has enabled the company to achieve higher margins, happier customers, and increased market share in the healthcare industry. By focusing on reducing waste, improving quality, and increasing efficiency, Virginia Mason Medical Center has been able to improve the patient experience and develop a reputation for high-quality care. The VMPS has allowed the company to reduce costs while improving patient safety and satisfaction, which has helped to increase market share and drive revenue growth.[v]

I once had a situation that needed drastic, immediate change. I took over an industry leader's highly technical product line that was producing their product at extremely low yields, the products were not highly reliable in the field with high warranty costs, cycle times were several months, and this was constricting the growth of the company. The mindset in the organization was that this was a very difficult product to make. The poor performance was to be expected. This attitude came from several exceptionally knowledgeable experts in the field as well as the people making this product. The expectations were very low on improving the situation. An attitude adjustment was sorely needed. What was required was a way to start a systematic approach to improve the performance, a Continuous Improvement System.

I could not accept this "fact" that this was the nature of this product. The actions I initiated led to breakthroughs that increased product yields, lowered product costs, improved cycle times, and allowed for the company to become the leader in their market niche. Of course, I had a lot of help in accomplishing these results. In addition to inheriting a highly skilled staff we hired new talented people, created new methods to find the source of defects, consolidated operations, and created a new culture driven to consistently improve the operation.

How did we do this? The actions were "commonsense" changes. I once sat in a meeting where the Quality Department was reviewing customer returns, Return Material Authorizations (RMAs), and this meeting was in its fifth hour with a long way to go before completing the full review of all these returns. I walked out of that meeting, before it ended, with a sick feeling in my stomach. I told the Senior Vice President that hired me that I would never sit through another meeting like that again. In that meeting, many of the status updates, on these RMAs, was that nothing was done to analyze the failure. Worse, in some cases the RMA was missing and couldn't be located. There was not an appreciation for the value that the RMAs had in providing feedback to improve the process. A large part of the ultimate success can be directly attributed to the analysis and improvements made directly from these RMAs.

The Continuous Improvement efforts in this operation began immediately after that meeting. The first step was to locate every single RMA and get them organized. I thought, what a gold mine these RMAs were! Here are field returns that contained the weaknesses in the various processes we used to build the product. We needed to analyze the complaints and find out what the root causes were. Once analyzed we could initiate corrective actions. I was almost giddy at the thought of having such a wonderful opportunity!

The steps taken to achieve the improvements were simple. You must start with standardized processes. Is your process documented? Do the people executing the process follow it, are they properly trained? We needed to eliminate and or minimize process variation so we could determine where and how a process is to be changed to yield improvements.

Next, we organized the process data, so it provided actionable information. We collected this data in an efficient manner and presented the results to the team responsible for the process. This included all facets of the business that has a stake in the results. Collecting the data is a process unto itself. Do you measure defects, do you drill down to process indicators, how is the data formatted? What are the best ways to present this data?

CHAPTER 6:

IMPLEMENTATION

We will now discuss how to implement a Continuous Improvement System. Implementing a Continuous Improvement System involves several steps, including identifying opportunities, developing plans, implementing improvement projects, and measuring and monitoring progress. Here's a breakdown of each step:

1. Identify opportunities: The first step in implementing a Continuous Improvement System is to identify areas where improvements can be made. This can be done through a variety of methods, including employee feedback, customer surveys, process mapping, and data analysis. Once opportunities are identified, they should be prioritized based on their potential impact and feasibility.

2. Develop plans: Once opportunities are identified, plans should be developed to address them. This involves defining the goals, objectives, and scope of the improvement project, as well as identifying the resources required and the timeline for implementation. Plans should also include a detailed description of the process or system being improved, as well as any potential risks or issues that may arise.

3. Implement improvement projects: With plans in place, improvement projects can be implemented. This involves executing the plan, making any necessary changes or adjustments along the way, and ensuring that the project stays on track and within budget. Communication is key

during this phase, and regular updates should be provided to all stakeholders to ensure that everyone is on the same page.

4. Measure and monitor progress: Once improvement projects are implemented, it is important to measure and monitor progress to ensure that the desired outcomes are being achieved. This involves collecting data, analyzing results, and making any necessary adjustments to the process or system. Key performance indicators (KPIs) should be established to track progress and ensure that the project is on track to meet its goals and objectives.

5. Continuously improve: The final step in implementing a Continuous Improvement System is to continuously improve. This involves using the data and feedback collected during the measurement and monitoring phase to identify new opportunities for improvement and make any necessary changes to the process or system. This is an ongoing process that requires a commitment to ongoing learning, collaboration, and innovation.

To ensure the success of a Continuous Improvement System, it is important to involve all stakeholders, from employees to customers to suppliers. This involves creating a culture of continuous improvement that fosters innovation, collaboration, and ongoing learning. It also requires a commitment from leadership to invest time, resources, and energy into continuous improvement initiatives and model the behaviors and values that are essential to a culture of continuous improvement.

Implementing a Continuous Improvement System involves several steps, including identifying opportunities, developing plans, implementing improvement projects, and measuring and monitoring progress. It is an ongoing process that requires a commitment to ongoing learning, collaboration, and innovation. By involving all stakeholders and creating a culture of continuous improvement, companies can improve efficiency, reduce waste, and enhance customer satisfaction. Continuous improvement is not a one-time event but rather a continuous process of identifying areas for improvement and making changes to achieve better results. It requires a commitment to ongoing learning and development, as well as a willingness to embrace change and try new approaches. The benefits of implementing a Continuous Improvement System are significant, including increased productivity, reduced costs, improved quality, and enhanced customer satisfaction. By following the steps outlined above and creating a culture of continuous improvement, companies can achieve long-term success and remain competitive in today's rapidly changing business environment.

CHAPTER 7:

THE IMPORTANCE OF DATA

Accurate data is also essential for measuring progress and evaluating the effectiveness of improvement efforts. In tracking key metrics over time, organizations can determine whether their improvement efforts are having the desired impact and allow them to make adjustments as needed. This helps to ensure that improvement efforts are focused on the areas that will have the greatest impact on the organization's overall performance.

Another benefit of accurate data is that it helps to ensure that improvement efforts are based on facts rather than assumptions or opinions. By collecting and analyzing data, organizations can avoid the biases and subjective judgments that can lead to ineffective improvements. This helps to ensure that improvement efforts are focused on the root causes of problems, rather than just treating symptoms.

Finally, accurate data is essential for effective communication and collaboration between employees. By sharing data with all stakeholders, organizations can ensure that everyone has a clear understanding of the organization's performance and the areas that require improvement. This helps to promote a culture of continuous improvement, where everyone is engaged and motivated to contribute to the organization's success.

Accurate data is essential for the success of a Continuous Improvement System. It provides the foundation for effective problem-solving, decision-making, and continuous improvement. By collecting and analyzing accurate data, organizations can identify areas for improvement, measure progress, evaluate the effectiveness of improvement efforts, avoid biases and subjective judgments, and promote effective communication and collaboration between employees.

A Continuous Improvement System requires various types of data to support its operations. Two essential types of data are Quality Data and Manufacturing Execution System (MES) data.

Quality Data refers to data that is collected to measure the quality of a product or service. This data includes information on defects, scrap rates, customer complaints, and other quality metrics. Quality data is essential for identifying areas for improvement in the production process and for tracking progress towards quality goals. For example, if a product has a high defect rate, quality data can be used to identify the root cause of the problem and implement corrective actions to reduce defects.

Manufacturing Execution System (MES) data refers to data that is collected from the production process. This data includes information on production rates, downtime, machine utilization, and other production metrics. MES data is essential for identifying areas for improvement in the production process and for tracking progress towards production goals. For example, if a production line is experiencing high downtime, MES data can be used to identify the root cause of the problem and implement corrective actions to reduce downtime.

Other types of data that are important for a Continuous Improvement System include financial data, customer data, and employee data. Financial data includes information on costs, revenues, and profits, and is essential for identifying areas for improvement in the organization's financial performance. Customer data includes information on customer satisfaction, loyalty, and complaints, and is essential for identifying areas for improvement in the organization's customer experience. Employee data includes information on employee satisfaction, turnover, and performance, and is essential for identifying areas for improvement in the organization's human resources practices.

In summary, Continuous Improvement Systems require various types of data to support its operations. Quality data and MES data are essential for identifying areas for improvement in the production process and for tracking progress towards quality and production goals. Other types of data, such as financial data, customer data, and employee data, are also important for identifying areas for improvement in other areas of the organization. By collecting and analyzing these types of data, organizations can identify areas for improvement, implement corrective actions, and continuously improve their performance.

CHAPTER 8:

CIS TOOLS AND TECHNIQUES

A Continuous Improvement System relies on a range of tools and techniques to identify areas for improvement and implement changes. Some of the commonly used tools and techniques include process mapping, root cause analysis, statistical process control, lean manufacturing, and Six Sigma.

Process mapping is a tool used to visually represent the steps in a process and identify areas where improvements can be made. When you map out the process, it is easier to identify inefficiencies, bottlenecks, and areas where errors or defects are likely to occur. This helps to identify areas for improvement and implement changes to improve the process.

Root cause analysis is a technique used to identify the underlying causes of a problem. By identifying the root cause of a problem, it is possible to implement corrective actions that will address the problem at its source. Root cause analysis involves asking a series of "why" questions to get to the underlying cause of the problem.

Statistical process control (SPC) is a technique used to monitor and control a process to ensure that it is operating within acceptable limits. SPC involves collecting data on key process variables and using statistical methods to analyze the data and identify trends or patterns. This helps to identify areas where the process is not operating within acceptable limits and implement corrective actions to bring the process back into control.

Lean is a philosophy and set of tools and techniques used to eliminate waste and improve efficiency in the production process. Lean manufacturing involves identifying and eliminating non-value-added activities, reducing cycle time, improving quality, and increasing efficiency. By implementing lean manufacturing principles, organizations can improve their competitiveness and profitability.

Six Sigma is a data-driven methodology used to improve quality and reduce defects in a process. Six Sigma involves defining the problem, measuring the process, analyzing the data, improving the process, and controlling the process. By following this methodology, organizations can identify areas for improvement, implement changes, and continuously improve their performance.

A Continuous Improvement System relies on a range of tools and techniques to identify areas for improvement and implement changes. Process mapping, root cause analysis, statistical process control, lean manufacturing, and Six Sigma are just a few of the tools and techniques used in a Continuous Improvement System. By using these tools and techniques, organizations can improve their efficiency, reduce waste, improve quality, and continuously improve their performance.

Another tool that I highly recommend is to make your data visible to everyone and updated regularly. Visual data can take many forms, including charts, graphs, dashboards, and scorecards. By presenting data in a visual format, it is easier to identify trends, patterns, and outliers that may not be immediately apparent when looking at raw data. This helps to identify areas for improvement and track progress towards improvement goals.

Visual data also promotes transparency and accountability within the organization. By making data available to everyone, it is easier to identify areas where performance is lagging and take action to address the problem. This helps to create a culture of continuous improvement, where everyone is engaged and motivated to contribute to the organization's success.

Another benefit of visual data is that it promotes effective communication and collaboration between employees. By sharing data with all stakeholders, everyone has a clear understanding of the organization's performance and the areas that require improvement. This helps to promote a culture of collaboration and teamwork, where everyone is working towards shared improvement goals.

Visual data helps to promote a sense of ownership and accountability among employees. When employees can see how their work contributes to the organization's overall performance, they are more likely to take ownership of their work and strive for excellence. This helps to improve employee engagement and motivation, and ultimately leads to better performance and results.

Having data visually available for everyone to see is essential for the success of a Continuous Improvement System. Visual data promotes transparency, accountability, effective communication, collaboration, and a sense of ownership among employees. By making data available in a visual format, organizations can identify areas for improvement, track progress towards improvement goals, and create a culture of continuous improvement.

CHAPTER 9:

THE BENEFITS

What are the benefits of implementing a Continuous Improvement System in your business? There are three main areas of benefits. The first are the benefits to the company. The second are benefits to your customers, clients, patients, or users based on your business. Lastly, there are benefits to your employees.

Implementing a Continuous Improvement System can provide numerous benefits to a company. By streamlining processes and eliminating waste, companies can increase productivity and output without increasing costs. Continuous improvement can help to reduce costs by eliminating waste, reducing errors, and improving efficiency. By identifying and addressing the root causes of quality issues, companies can improve the overall quality of their products or services, resulting in increased customer satisfaction and loyalty. By improving quality, reducing lead times, and providing better customer service, companies can enhance customer satisfaction and loyalty, leading to increased sales and revenue.

Continuous improvement initiatives can help to engage employees by providing opportunities for feedback, collaboration, and innovation. This can lead to increased job satisfaction, motivation, and retention. By encouraging a culture of continuous improvement, companies can foster innovation and creativity, leading to new products, services, and processes that can give them a competitive advantage in the marketplace. By collecting and analyzing data, companies can make better-informed decisions about their operations, resulting in improved efficiency and effectiveness.

Continuous improvement can help companies to respond quickly to changes in the marketplace, customer needs, and emerging technologies, allowing them to adapt and remain competitive. Documenting processes and tracking progress, companies can increase transparency and accountability, leading to greater trust and confidence among stakeholders. This can also help to improve risk management practices by identifying and addressing potential risks and issues, reducing the likelihood of legal or financial penalties, and ensuring compliance with regulatory requirements.

Implementing a Continuous Improvement System can provide numerous benefits to a company, including increased productivity, reduced costs, improved quality, enhanced customer satisfaction, improved employee engagement, increased innovation, better decision-making, increased agility, greater transparency, and improved risk management. In creating a culture of continuous improvement, companies can improve their operations, remain competitive, and achieve long-term success.

A Continuous Improvement System can provide significant added value benefits for customers. By improving the quality of products or services, companies can reduce defects and errors, leading to increased customer satisfaction and loyalty. Faster service can also be provided by streamlining processes and eliminating waste, which can reduce lead times and improve responsiveness. This can help companies to better meet the needs of their customers and provide a competitive advantage in the marketplace.

Better customer service is another added value benefit that a Continuous Improvement System can provide. By improving processes and providing better training to employees, companies can provide better customer service, resulting in increased satisfaction and loyalty. Customized products or services can also be developed through continuous improvement. By better understanding customer needs and preferences, companies can develop customized products or services that meet their specific requirements. This can lead to increased customer satisfaction and loyalty, as well as a competitive advantage in the marketplace.

Competitive pricing is another added value benefit that a Continuous Improvement System can provide for customers. By reducing costs through continuous improvement, companies can offer competitive pricing to customers, making their products or services more attractive in the marketplace. This can help to differentiate the company from competitors and increase sales and revenue.

Finally, enhanced communication is an added value benefit that a Continuous Improvement System can provide for customers. In implementing a Continuous Improvement System, companies can improve communication with customers, providing regular updates on products or services and responding more quickly to customer inquiries and concerns. This can lead to increased customer satisfaction and loyalty, as well as a better understanding of customer needs and preferences.

A Continuous Improvement System can also provide significant benefits to employees. One of the most significant benefits is improved morale. Continuous Improvement initiatives can help to engage employees by providing opportunities for feedback, collaboration, and innovation. This can lead to increased job satisfaction, motivation, and retention. When employees feel that their input is valued and that they are part of the solution, they are more likely to be engaged and committed to the company's success.

One of the most important advantages is increased job satisfaction. When employees are involved in the improvement process, they feel more valued and engaged in their work, which can lead to higher motivation and job satisfaction.

Continuous improvement also provides opportunities for employees to develop new skills and techniques that can help them grow professionally and become more valuable to the organization. This can lead to career growth opportunities and a sense of pride and ownership in their work.

Another benefit of continuous improvement is improved communication and collaboration between employees. Working together towards shared goals can improve relationships and communication, which can lead to a more positive work environment.

Continuous improvement can also lead to a safer and healthier work environment, which can improve employee well-being and reduce the risk of workplace accidents or injuries. Additionally, employees who contribute to the success of the continuous improvement system may be recognized and rewarded for their efforts, boosting morale and motivation.

Overall, implementing a continuous improvement system can provide numerous benefits for employees, including increased job satisfaction, skill development, career growth opportunities, improved communication and collaboration, increased safety and well-being, recognition and rewards, a greater sense of ownership, enhanced problem-solving skills, and improved work-life balance.

CHAPTER 10:

THE LIMITATIONS

There are limitations to Continuous Improvement Systems. The focus of Continuous Improvement is on existing processes. These are often restricted by process capabilities, software limitations, capital equipment, available technology when the process was first developed, and a company's financial position and restrictions.

If the Strategic Objectives for your business are beyond the capabilities of these current processes more than a Continuous Improvement System will be required to achieve these goals. It will take a leap from the current process capabilities that include Capital Expenditure Budget (CAPEX) on equipment and software.

It is important to remember that a Continuous Improvement System maximizes the capabilities within existing processes. Overall Performance Improvement is a topic for another discussion, but it is sufficient to state that future course adjustments for the business are usually outside the scope of a Continuous Improvement System. The results of a mature Continuous Improvement System may lead to an understanding that the current processes do not enable the Business to achieve their Strategic Goals.

It is imperative that you and your team develop the Continuous Improvement mindset. People always are the key factor in the success or failure of any system. You want to select people that feel they have a "career" and that getting better every-day is critical to both their own and your company's success. People that view their effort at work as a "job" tend to be resistant to change. They want to work their 8 hours and collect a paycheck.

It is your job as the owner or leader to create the vision of what the future will look like. The Continuous Improvement System is a tool to achieve the business's strategic objectives. It is extremely important that the strategic objectives are aligned with the KPI's that you elect to track at the outset. Further, communication to your team members as to why you are implementing a Continuous Improvement System and your expectations will create the vision.

Implementing a continuous improvement system can bring significant benefits to an organization, but it is not without its limitations. One of the biggest challenges is getting employees to buy into the system and actively participate in the improvement process. This can be difficult if employees are resistant to change or do not see the value in the system.

Another limitation is the cost and time involved in implementing a continuous improvement system. It can require significant investment in training, infrastructure, and technology, which may not be feasible for all organizations. Additionally, the process of continuous improvement can be time-consuming and may take resources away from other important areas of the business.

One of the biggest risks of implementing a continuous improvement system is that it can become too focused on efficiency and cost-cutting, at the expense of other important factors such as quality, safety, and employee well-being. This can lead to a negative work environment and decreased employee morale.

The success of a continuous improvement system relies on accurate data and metrics to measure progress and identify areas for improvement. If the data is incomplete or inaccurate, it can lead to misguided decisions and ineffective improvements.

While implementing a continuous improvement system can bring significant benefits, it is important to be aware of the potential limitations and risks involved in the process. Careful planning, communication, and employee engagement can help mitigate these risks and ensure the success of the system.

CHAPTER 11:

CONCLUSION

Instituting a Continuous Improvement System is within the grasp of all businesses. The concept is commonsense approach to organizing a process control with a feedback loop. This feedback loop, the data, feeds the changes to the process that creates Continuous Improvement.

You do not need to be a PhD in Statistics to start a Continuous Improvement System in your business. Starting a Continuous Improvement System in your business will put you on a path to improve the process performance. Once on that path you can learn more and decide which way to take your efforts in the future.

Building a culture that thrives in a Continuous Improvement System is a key factor in growing your company. You need to select personnel that have this "open" mindset to grow. It is human nature to resist change. The Continuous Improvement System thrives in an environment of constant changes. This is the human challenge that faces companies embracing this approach. Continuous Improvement, to be successful, must be embedded in the Company Culture, the "How we do things here" mindset required to reap the full benefits of the Continuous Improvement System.

There are several future trends in Continuous Improvement Systems that are likely to shape the way organizations approach improvement in the coming years.

One of the most significant trends is the increasing use of digital technologies to support continuous improvement. This includes the use of data analytics, artificial intelligence, and machine learning to identify patterns and opportunities for improvement. Organizations are also using digital platforms and tools to facilitate collaboration and communication between employees, and to track progress and measure results.

Another trend is the growing emphasis on sustainability and social responsibility in continuous improvement. Organizations are increasingly recognizing the importance of considering the environmental and social impact of their operations. They are incorporating these considerations into their improvement efforts. This includes reducing waste, reducing energy consumption, and promoting social and environmental responsibility throughout the supply chain.

A third trend is the focus on agility and flexibility in continuous improvement. Organizations are recognizing the need to be able to adapt quickly to changes in the market and respond to new challenges and opportunities. This requires a more agile approach to improvement, with a focus on rapid experimentation, testing, and learning.

There is a growing recognition of the importance of employee engagement and empowerment in continuous improvement. Organizations are realizing that employees are the key to successful improvement efforts, and are investing in training, development, and communication to ensure that employees are fully engaged and motivated to participate in the process.

The future of Continuous Improvement Systems is likely to be characterized by a greater emphasis on digital technologies, sustainability and social responsibility, agility and flexibility, and employee engagement and empowerment. By embracing these trends, organizations can ensure that they remain competitive and responsive in a rapidly changing business environment.

You now have a choice. This is the decision to implement a Continuous Improvement System in your company. You can start on this path today. You can add this as a Strategic Objective to help your business survive for now and to thrive in the future. You can become part of a new study in the future. Your company can be added to the list of companies that faced their Defining Moment and chose to launch their efforts to begin their journey of Continuous Improvement. It is down to you, please make the right decision. Your company's future depends on it.

Larry Ibbetson can be found at Ibbetson Performance Consulting LLC at

https://www.IbbetsonPerformance.com

[i] References:Institute for Healthcare Improvement. (2021). ContinuousImprovement.
http://www.ihi.org/resources/Pages/ImprovementStories/ContinuousImprovement.aspx

International Organization for Standardization. (2015). ISO 9000:2015 Quality management systems - Fundamentals and vocabulary. https://www.iso.org/standard/62085.html

[ii] 1. Feigenbaum, A. (1951). Total Quality Control. McGraw-Hill Education.

2. Dale, B. G. (1994). Managing Quality. Prentice Hall.

3. Juran, J. M., & Gryna, F. M. (1993). Quality Planning and Analysis: From Product Development through Use. McGraw-Hill Education.

4. Womack, J. P., Jones, D. T., & Roos, D. (1990). The Machine That Changed the World: The Story of Lean Production. Free Press.

[iii] Liker, J. K. (2004). The Toyota Way: 14 Management Principles from the World's Greatest Manufacturer. McGraw-Hill Professional.

[iv] Southwest Airlines. (2021). Our Purpose and Vision https://www.southwest.com/html/about-southwest/index.html

[v] Virginia Mason Medical Center. (2021). Virginia Mason ProductionSystem.
https://www.virginiamason.org/virginia-mason-production-system

Gardner, P. (2010). Virginia Mason Medical Center: Achieving Excellence. Healthcare Executive, 25(6), 32-35.

www.ingramcontent.com/pod-product-compliance
Lightning Source LLC
Chambersburg PA
CBHW072025230526
45466CB00019B/815